MATLAB
Getting Started in
4 Hours

Gayan Illeperuma

ISBN- 9798862286793

DEDICATED TO MY FAMILY

Content

Introduction

Software can take years to master. With MATLAB, being complex software, there could still be new things to learn, even after years of usage.

However, sometimes mastery is not what you seek. When the deadline of a research project is coming closer or when you only need to perform a 'very simple task', you will want to get it done as quickly as possible. Usually in situations like that, you do not have enough time to learn in depth about all the functions of the software. What you need then is a quick guide to the most commonly used functions. This book is intended for such an audience. We will get the essentials covered very quickly and get you off the ground as fast as possible.

If you have more free time and wish to study MATLAB in greater detail, look for my other book "MATLAB, a Detailed Guide for Beginners".

For years, I had been teaching an undergraduate course for freshmen that required extensive programming skills. Most of these students did not have prior experience with MATLAB or computer programming. Therefore, the first lecture was usually about getting started with MATLAB programming. Mastering MATLAB in the limited 4-hour period was impractical. However, it was enough time to teach the students the basics, so they could tackle most common problems. In an average MATLAB program, over 90% of the code consists of less than a dozen key words.

So, if they can do it so can you! Let's dive in...

This book is organized as a collection of several chapters. In the introduction, you will learn the structure of the book and how to use it.

Chapter 1 is dedicated to getting your feet wet. It will introduce the graphical user interface and basic usage of menus, windows, and icons in the MATLAB software. If you haven't installed the software yet, you will be able to find information on how to install it in the appendix. By the end of chapter 2, you will know what most of the windows are used for.

Chapter 2 is dedicated to arithmetic operations. Here, you will learn how to use MATLAB as an advanced calculator. You will also learn about matrices and variables. At the end of this chapter, you will be able to use MATLAB for arithmetic operations and matrix manipulations.

In *Chapter 3,* you will learn about writing a MATLAB script, which is a collection of a batch of commands. You will also start to learn more about variables.

In *Chapter 4,* you will begin to learn how to use MATLAB as a programming tool. You will learn about basic syntax of programming. This is a major chapter.

Chapter 5 is dedicated to symbolic mathematics. You will learn everything from solving simultaneous equations to differentiation and integration.

Chapter 6 includes details about different types of graphs. These include bar graphs, line charts histograms, and many more.

Lastly, we have an introduction to advance concepts and a list of references, where you can learn many other features.

Except for the first one, all the chapters are organized in the same format. We start by giving you a brief introduction on what you are going to learn by the end. We start with simple syntax and gradually increase the complexity. Each step is followed by a set of examples and exercises.

Chapter 1 : Getting started

Graphical User Interface

The version of MATLAB we are using is **MATLAB 2013b**. However, newer versions have almost identical commands and a very similar user interface.

First, start the program by clicking the MATLAB icon on the desktop or going through the start menu. It may take some time for the program to load completely into the memory. Once it is fully loaded, the Graphical User Interface (GUI) will appear and it will look like

Figure 1-1.

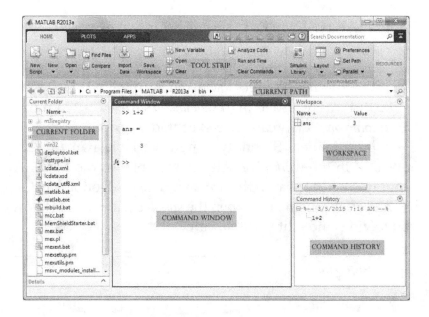

Figure 1-1 MATLAB GUI

If the status bar at the bottom left says *initializing*, you may have to wait few more minutes. If your GUI looks different, set it to default view by following this menu path:

Home - > Layout - > Default

Each sub window in the software will have its name on the title bar. In the *command window* you will see an indicator similar to ">>". This means that MATLAB is waiting for your commands. Click on that location and type the following

```
>> 1 + 2
```

Now press the *Enter* key. You will be greeted by the answer.

```
ans =
3
```

Congratulations! You just finished your first exercise.

Aside from the answer appearing on the *command window*, two other changes occurred in the GUI. First, your command was recorded in the *command history*. Any command in the *command history* can be re-executed by double clicking on the relevant line. Secondly a new variable named "ans" appeared in the *Workspace*. All the variables in the MATLAB programs will appear in the *workspace window*. Double-clicking on the variable name will open the *variable editor*, which allows you to view and edit variable values.

> ***Important***

MATLAB is case sensitive; therefore, do not interchange uppercase and lowercase letters in commands or variable names.

Arithmetic Operations

Using what you learned in the previous exercise, you should be able to do simple arithmetic from *command window* now.

Table 1-1 provides syntax for the most commonly used arithmetic operations.

Operation	Syntax	Example
Addition	+	1+2
Subtraction	-	5-3
Multiplication	*	2*3
Division	/	10/2
Square root	sqrt()	sqrt(25)
Power	^	10^2

Table 1-1 common arithmetic operations

A more complete list of arithmetic operators can be found in the appendix of the book.

Exercise

1) $3 + 5$

2) $1 - 5$

3) $2 + 4 \times 3$

4) $(2 + 4) \times 3$

5) $\sqrt{4}$

6) $\sqrt{-4}$

Precedence

Precedence is the order according to which arithmetic operations are performed. When calculating $2 + 4 \times 3$, multiplication is done prior to addition because multiplication has a higher precedence than addition. Following is a list of operations in order from higher precedence to lower precedence.

1. Parentheses ()
2. Transpose (.'), power (^)
3. Unary plus (+), unary minus (-). Do not confuse these with addition and subtraction.
4. Multiplication (*), division (/)
5. Addition (+), subtraction (-)

For a more complete list, please refer to the appendix at the end.

Using the parentheses, you can force a change in the order in which operations are calculated.

Example

Calculate $\frac{12+9}{3}$

It is clear that 5 and 4 need to be added first and that the result should be divided by the 3. A student may forget about precedence and try something like

```
>> 12+9/3
```

Since division has higher precedence than addition, it should be calculated first. The intermediate step would be $12 + 3$, which is not what we intended. The final answer would be

```
ans   =
15
```

This is an **incorrect** answer. The correct calculation should be

```
>> (12 + 9)/3
```

Since parentheses have a higher precedence, the addition would be done first. The intermediate step would be $21/3$, and the final result would be

```
ans   =
15
```

which is the correct answer.

Important:

When there are nested parentheses, calculation would start from the inner most parenthesis and move outward.

Practice exercises

Calculate the following expressions

1) $\frac{(2+4)}{5} \times 3$

2) $-0.25 + 10 \times 3$

3) $(3 + 4i)^3$

4) $2\pi \times 10$

5) $\frac{-b \pm \sqrt{b^2 - 4ac}}{2a}$ Where a = 10 b = 20 and c = 6

6) $2 \sin\frac{1}{2}(\alpha + \beta) \cos\frac{1}{2}(\alpha - \beta)$ Where $\alpha = 0.22$ and $\beta = 0.34$

Tip 1

MATLAB has a collection of commonly used constants. They may be called by their name. For example, to calculate $2 \times \pi$ we can use

>> 2*pi

MATLAB would automatically replace pi with 3.14... In the appendix you can find a more complete list of built-in MATLAB constants and operators.

A common mistake beginners make is to use

>>2pi

This would produce an error. It is always required to use an operator between operands. Use 2*pi instead.

Tip 2

Very large numbers and very small numbers can easily be written using normalized scientific notation. In normalized scientific notation, any number is written in the form $a \times 10^b$ Where a is between 1 and 10 and b is an integer.

E.g.

1200 is written as 1.2×10^3

0.0001 is written as 1.0×10^{-4}

In MATLAB, powers of ten are represented by the letter E

in MATLAB terms

>> 1.2E3

would mean 1200.

You can use a negative sign with E.

TIP 3

Unlike many other programming languages, MATLAB is built to handle mathematics. If you try an expression like 1/0 in JAVA, C, PHP or many other programming languages, a 'division by zero' error would occur.

However, MATLAB would correctly calculate it to infinity which is displayed as *Inf*. Any undefined value would be represented by *NaN*, which stands for Not a Number.

But MATLAB still has limitations on the maximum and minimum size of numbers it can store. If a number is extremely large, it may approximate to infinity. If a number is extremely small, it may be rounded off to zero. Finding ways of overcoming this is beyond the scope of this book.

Tip 4

Soon, your command window will be filled with old commands. Use the `clc` command to clean the command window

Exercises 2

1) Radius of a circle is 2.5 cm. Calculate its circumference and area.
   ($C = 2\pi r, A = \pi r^2$)

2) 16 g of oxygen contains 6.022×10^{23} oxygen atoms. How many oxygen atoms would be in 100 g of oxygen?

3) If the speed of light is 3×10^8 meters per second, how far will light travel in a year? How long will it take for a light beam to reach the moon from the earth? (The average distance between the earth and the moon is 384,400 km)

4) 1 ml of human blood contains an average of 5 billion (5×10^9) red blood cells. Each is doughnut shaped and has an average diameter of 6 µm (6×10^{-6}). If a person has 4.7 l of blood, what would be the length of the string made by putting all his blood cells in a row, touching each other?

5) A person deposits USD 1000 in a bank with an interest rate of 1.23 per year. Calculate the total earnings at the end of the 5th year.

6) Multiply 1.1 by itself 100 times.

7) Multiply 1.1 by itself one million times. How do you explain the result?

Chapter 2 : Writing Scripts

Introduction

In the last chapter, we learned how to use the command window to perform arithmetic operations. However, this method soon becomes tiresome as the calculations become more and more complex and consist of multiple steps. Another disadvantage is the inability to save the commands for sharing or later usage.

MATLAB scripts provide solutions to the above problems. Simply put, Script is a set of MATLAB commands stored in a file.

Creating a Script File

To start a new script file, use the following menu path **HOME -> NEW -> Script.**

A new window called *Editor* will appear with a blank script file. At the same time, *editor tool strip* will become visible (See Figure 2-1).

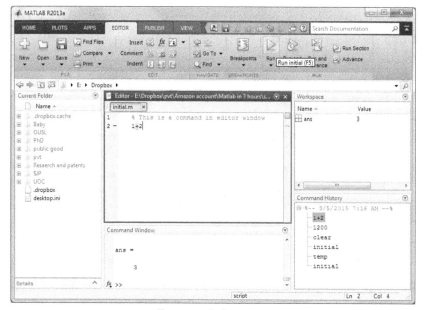

Figure 2-1 Editor window

In the editor, type

```
1+2
```

Such a command is known as a *statement* in computer programming jargon. A statement is the smallest meaningful unit in computer instruction. A computer program is made from multiple statements.

Using the menu path **Editor -> Save -> Save As**, save the file.

Do not use keywords as file names or include spaces within the file name. File names can only contain numbers, letters or hyphens (_) and cannot start with a number.

Unlike in the command window, the code you wrote will not be calculated until you *run* the file. To run the file, click the run icon (looks like a large green play button, Figure 2-2) in the editor tool bar. Alternatively, you can use the *F5* function key as a key board shortcut.

Figure 2-2 Run icon

If the location where you save the script is different from the MATLAB current path, a window will pop up to ask you how to proceed. The options will include adding the path and changing the current folder. Select the *change folder* option.

If everything is successful, you will see an answer appear in the command window.

```
    ans   =
15
```

You can use any command used in the command window to build *statements* in the scripts. A single script can have many statements.

E.g.

```
    1+2
5*pi/(10)
sqrt(4)
```

Each of the statements in the above script will be calculated in order, and the results will appear in the command window.

```
ans =
      3

ans =
      1.5708

ans =
      2
```

TIP

As you run multiple scripts, it will not be long before all your workspace and the command window is filled by unused variables and results. The following commands clean the *workspace* and the *command window*, respectively. It is good practice to use them at the **beginning** of the script files.

clear
clc

Exercise

1. Repeat the exercises in the above chapter using scripts.

Variables

A variable is like a box where you can store a value. In programming terms, storing a value to a variable is called *assigning*. Syntax of the assignation mark is "="

E.g.

```
a = 10
```

would instruct MATLAB to store value 10 in the box labeled as 'A'. (In programming terms, it would assign the value 10 to the variable A.)

Important

It is always the value on the **right-hand side** of the assignation mark that is calculated, and the result is assigned to the left-hand side of the variable. This is different from the mathematical equal sign, which is symmetrical.

So syntax like
10 = a
is invalid in programming, since you cannot put a variable to a number. (A ball can be put into a box, but not the other way around).

You can issue generic commands like adding two boxes. Depending on the values in the boxes (variables), your output would be different. For example, the output of

```
a + b
```

would be different depending on the values stored on the variables 'a' and 'b'

Example

```
radius = 10
```

In the above statement, we are creating a variable named *radius* and assigning a value of 10 to it.

TIP 1

> Boxes come in various sizes and shapes. Not every box is suitable to store all the different objects. Similarly, there are different types of variables. By default, MATLAB is intelligent enough to automatically select the best variable type. But in some cases, you can change the variable type manually.

Naming variables

MATLAB variable names are case sensitive. Therefore, *myvar* and *MYvar* would be considered two different variables. A variable name cannot have spaces and cannot begin with numbers. Reserved keywords such as *exit, clc* cannot be used as variable names.

Once a value is assigned to a variable, it can be used in other statements.

```
    radius = 10
pi*radius^2
```

When MATLAB calculates the second statement, radius will be replaced by 10. The above example can be expanded as follows.

```
    radius = 10
cost_per_unit_area = 0.2

area = pi*radius^2
total_cost = area*cost_per_unit_area
```

In the above example, *radius* and *cost_per_unit_area* are variables, and values of 10 and 0.2 are assigned. The *area* and *total_cost* are calculated based on the value of *radius*.

If the radius is changed, we only need to change the first statement and run the script again. *area* and *total_cost* will be recalculated using the new *radius* value. This flexibility is one major advantage of using scripts.

Comments

Comments do not affect the execution of the program. Their purpose is to provide the programmer with a convenient, short documentation method. Comments can be used to provide generic information, such as author name and revision date for the program, or they can be more specific inline comments that describe statements in the program.

In MATLAB, comments start with a % sign and end at the end of line. MATLAB does not have multiline commenting or a special comment ending syntax. Therefore, any text starting from the comment sign to the end of the line would be a comment and would not be evaluated. Commented text is displayed in green.

Example

```
% This is my first program.
% It was written in 2015
% GNU copyright
    clear % clean the workspace variables
    clc   % this command deletes all the
previous results in workspace
```

```
r = 10 % this is the radius of the circle
   % following section calculate the area
area = pi*radius^2
```

Suppressing Output

So far, the output of all the statements was printed on the command window. It is more convenient to print only the important results. Suppressing the output of any statement can be achieved by putting a semicolon (;) sign at the end of the statement.

Example

```
radius = 10 %this will be printed
cost_per_unit = 0.2;  %this will not be printed
area = pi*radius^2;
total_cost = area*area
```

In the above script, the third and fourth lines end with a semicolon. Therefore, output from these lines is not printed in the command window. Only the following output will be printed.

```
   radius =
10
total_cost =
9.8696e+04
```

Exercise

1) Write a script to calculate the volume and surface area of a cube.

2) A box contains half a dozen eggs. Write a program to assign the weight of each egg to a variable. Calculate the average weight of an egg.

3) A cylindrical tank has a radius of 2m and a height of 5m. Calculate its volume and assign it to a variable. If the tank is filled at a rate of 0.5 m^3s^{-1}, how long will it take to fill the tank? Use variables and comments when appropriate.

4) A scanner has 300 dots per inch. The shape of a square with 2-inch sides is scanned. How many pixels will it cover?

Chapter 3 : Matrices

Introduction

Matrix is a very important concept in mathematics. Inside MATLAB, most variables are represented as a matrix. Some operations can be accomplished easily when presented in the matrix format. Therefore, it is important to learn basic concepts of matrices and how to use them inside MATLAB.

A matrix can be thought of as a table where each cell is a variable. The number of rows and the number of columns in a matrix are called the order of the matrix.

Example

$$\begin{bmatrix} 4 & 0 & 2 \\ 6 & 5 & 6 \end{bmatrix}$$

The above matrix has an order of 2x3. By default, the row number is stated before the column number.

All the cells must hold the same data type. A single cell is sometimes known as an element. A single variable name is used to identify the matrix. The value in each cell can be accessed individually by giving its location using row number and column number.

TIP

If you wish to save different data types or you need a more complex structure (non-rectangular or cascading), you have to use MATLAB structures.

Creating A Matrix

In MATLAB, a matrix is defined using square brackets. Commas or spaces separate elements in the same row. Rows are separated using semicolons.

Example

Let's create the following matrix A.

$$A = \begin{bmatrix} 5 & 4 & 2 \\ 0 & 6 & 6 \\ 4 & 2 & 1 \end{bmatrix}$$

To create the above matrix in MATLAB and assign it to the variable A, the following command can be used

```
>> A = [5 4 2;0 6 6;4 2 1]
A =
        5       4       2
        0       6       6
        4       2       1
```

In the *workspace*, you will notice the new variable A. If you double-click on it, the *variable window* will open, and values in the matrix can be seen (Figure 3-1). You can easily edit the matrix within the *variable window*.

Figure 3-1Matrix in variable editor and workspace

To access an element in a matrix, use the matrix name followed by the location of the element. In MATLAB notations, the row number comes first, followed by the column number.

Example

Let's try to access the top right corner element of the above matrix A. Its location is 1st row and 3rd column. Therefore, the command is

```
>> A(1,3)
```

which gives the result

```
>>Ans
```
2

To call the element in the center

```
>> A(2,2)
```

Let us try to call all the elements in the second row. To represent "all columns" we would replace the column number with a colon (:).

Example

Let us access all the elements in the second row.

```
>> A(2,:)
ans =
     0    6    6
```

In this same way, we can select all the elements in a given column. Here we would replace the row number with the colon.

Example

Let's try to call all the elements in the first row.

```
>>  A(:,1)
ans =
     5
     0
     4
```

Calling a Range of Elements

For this example, we need a large matrix. The `magic` command creates a magic square with a given size, and we will use it instead of typing all the elements.

```
>> my_mat = magic(10)
```

```
my_mat =

    92    99     1     8    15    67    74    51    58    40
    98    80     7    14    16    73    55    57    64    41
     4    81    88    20    22    54    56    63    70    47
    85    87    19    21     3    60    62    69    71    28
    86    93    25     2     9    61    68    75    52    34
    17    24    76    83    90    42    49    26    33    65
    23     5    82    89    91    48    30    32    39    66
    79     6    13    95    97    29    31    38    45    72
    10    12    94    96    78    35    37    44    46    53
    11    18   100    77    84    36    43    50    27    59
```

Let's select elements from the 3rd column to the 5th column in the 2nd row. Since the row number is given first, it is written immediately after the matrix name. The range is given in the format *starting location : ending location*.

```
>> my_range = my_mat( 2 , 3:5)
my_range =
     7    14    16
```

The following example selects the first five rows and the first three columns.

```
my_range = my_mat( 1:5 , 1:3)
```

Detecting Size of Matrix

There are many situations, where the number of rows and columns needs to be detected. The keyword `size` can be used for this.

Example

```
>> A = [1 2 3;4 5 6]
A =

     1     2     3
     4     5     6
```

```
>> size(A)
ans =
     2     3
```

By default, it will show the number of rows and columns (and any other dimensions) in order. A second parameter can be used if only one dimension is required. 1 is used for rows , 2 is used for columns.

```
>> size(A,1)
ans =
     2
```

You can use the keyword end to refer to the last element of the matrix. The following command will select the last five elements in the first row

A(1,end-5:end)

A common error made by many is trying to access a non-existing element. For example, if matrix A has only 5 rows but you call A(6), it will create an error. Since there isn't a 6th element, this error is known as a matrix out of bound error.

Editing Matrices

When updating an element in a matrix, we would assign the new value to the proper location of the matrix.

Example

Let's create a matrix first

```
>> A = [5 4 2;0 6 6;4 2 1]
```

Now change the value at location 2,2 to 10.

```
>> A (2,2) = 10

A =

        5       4       2
        0      10       6
        4       2       1
```

Removing a Column / Row

To remove a column or a row, we simply assign an empty matrix to that column or row.

An empty matrix is a matrix without any elements. It is coded as [ ].

Let's try to delete the second column in the above matrix A.

```
>> A(:,2) = []
A =
        5       2
        0       6
        4       1
```

Concatenating Matrices

Concatenation is the appending of two matrices to create one larger matrix. The final matrix should still obey all the limitations of the matrices. Therefore, they need to have the same data type. Depending on the dimension of concatenation, the number of rows or columns needs to be equal.

It is possible to use parentheses or the keyword `cat` for concatenations.

Example

Let A and B be two matrices as below

```
>> A = [1 2 3;4 5 6]
B = [7,8,9;10,11,12]

A =
        1       2       3
        4       5       6

B =
        7       8       9
       10      11      12
```

Concatenate horizontally

```
>> C = [A B]

C =
        1       2       3       7       8       9
        4       5       6      10      11      12
```

Concatenate vertically

```
>> C = [A; B]
```

C =

1	2	3
4	5	6
7	8	9
10	11	12

With a loop structure, this method can be used easily to append new data to a matrix.

Exercise

1) Create the following matrix

$$A = \begin{bmatrix} 1 & 3 & 8 \\ 5 & 4 & 2 \\ 2 & 4 & 6 \end{bmatrix}$$

2) Select the second element in the first row.

3) Select all the elements in the second row and assign them to matrix B

4) Replace the center cell of matrix A with 0

5) Remove the 3rd column from matrix B

Matrix Arithmetic

Matrix arithmetic is slightly different from scalar arithmetic. The following is a list of commands and examples.

$$\text{Let } A = \begin{bmatrix} 1 & 3 & 8 \\ 5 & 4 & 2 \\ 2 & 4 & 6 \end{bmatrix} \quad B = \begin{bmatrix} 6 & 2 & 0 \\ 2 & -3 & 0 \\ 6 & 3 & 3 \end{bmatrix} \quad C = \begin{bmatrix} 2 \\ 6 \\ 8 \end{bmatrix}$$

Operation	Syntax	Example
Addition	+	A+B
Subtraction	-	A-B
Matrix Multiplication	*	A*B
Matrix Transpose	' or transpose()	A'
Determinant	det()	det(B)
Inverse	inv	Inv(A)

For a more complete list, please refer to the appendix

Array Operations

Aside from Matrix operations, MATLAB has array operations (vector operations). These operate on each element separately

Operation	Syntax	Example
Element wise product	.*	A .*B
Element wise power	.^	A.^2

The following example illustrates the difference between these two types of operations

$$\text{Let } A = \begin{bmatrix} 1 & 3 & 8 \\ 5 & 4 & 2 \\ 2 & 4 & 6 \end{bmatrix}$$

The first command will calculate the square of the matrix, like multiplying two matrices.

```
A^2  =        32      47      62
              29      39      60
              34      46      60
```

The following instruction will square each element separately. Therefore, A can be of any size.

```
A.^2  =
              1        9      64
             25       16       4
              4       16      36
```

Chapter 4 : Programming

Introduction to Programming

A computer program is a set of instructions given to a computer about how to perform a task. These instructions are written in special languages known as computer languages. The grammar and other rules of a particular language are known as the syntax of the language. Although some syntax may be different, most computer languages follow a similar underline design.

Here are some of the rules in MATLAB.

- A single instruction is known as a statement. In general, each statement is written on a separate line. (See appendix for exceptions)

- You can have empty lines between statements and they will be ignored.

- Base words which form the language (E.g. `clear`, `load`) are called keywords. A keyword cannot be used as a variable name or a file name.

- MATLAB is case sensitive. All the keywords, variable names etc. must be in the correct case.

- In general, programs are executed sequentially. I.e. each statement is evaluated one after another, in order.

- The symbol = is called the assignation mark. It instructs the computer to evaluate the right side and assign the result to the left side variable. It is different from the equal sign in mathematics.

  x = x +1 is interpreted as calculate x + 1, then assign result to x. But in mathematics, the above statement is a contradiction.

  Now let's see an example of the above rules

Example

Maximum height reached by a projected ball is given by following equations.

$$vertical\ velocity = speed \times sine\ (projected\ angle)$$
$$maximum\ height = \frac{vertical\ velocity^2}{2g}$$

If the initial speed is 10 and the projected angle is 60^0, it can be coded in MATLAB as follows. Comments are added to explain different sections.

```
% clean the workspace
clear
clc

% start of the program
% Following data is provided

projected_speed = 10;
projected_angle = pi/3;
g = 9.8;
% Lets do the calculation itself
```

```
vertical_velocity =
projected_speed*sin(projected_angle);
    maximum_height = vertical_velocity^2/ (2*g)
```

Here, each step is calculated in order. First, the workspace is cleared of any leftover values. It is a good habit to get into. Then three variables are created for storing angle, project speed, and g. At the same time, they are assigned the values indicated in the problem. Next, the calculation is carried out. First, vertical velocity is calculated and it is assigned to a variable named vertical_velocity. This variable is used to calculate the maximum height. Display of intermediate results is suppressed using semicolons.

Values of the two parameters, *projected_speed* and *projected_angle*, are built into the program. Therefore, they are known as hard-coded values.

It may be more convenient if these values were extracted from user rather than being hard-coded.

Getting Keyboard Input

As mentioned earlier, hard-coded values are 'hard to change'. You need to change the actual program each time. Let's modify the program so a person can enter a value for a variable using the key board. This method allows someone to change the values without changing the program.

The following is the syntax for getting keyboard input and assigning it to a variable.

```
variable_name = input ('text displayed to
the user')
```

To match the above example, we may use.

```
projected_speed = input('Please enter the
speed \n');
```

\n is called an escape character. It moves the cursor to a new line. Refer to appendix for a more complete list. The modified code would look like

```
clear
clc

%lets get speed from keyboard
projected_speed = input('Please enter the
speed \n');
projected_angle = pi/3;
g = 9.8;

vertical_velocity =
projected_speed*sin(projected_angle);
maximum_height = vertical_velocity^2/ (2*g)
```

When the program is executed, it will display input message and wait for user to provide input at the command line. Once the user types a value and presses the enter key, it will be assigned to the parameter and the program will resume running.

```
>> Please enter the speed
25
maximum_height =
    23.9158
```

Exercise

1) Modify the above program to get both speed and the angle from keyboard.

2) Write a MATLAB program to calculate the surface area and the volume of a sphere when value of radius is given from a keyboard

3) Store 3 values entered from keyboard in a matrix. Display their average value.

Displaying Results

Sometimes it is required to display the results within a sentence. (E.g. "The speed of the particle is 23 km/h"). We can do this by printing the result to the command line. `sprintf`, and `fprintf` are two commands that can be used for this purpose.

Example

```
fprintf ('this is a test program.')
```

would display
```
this is a test program.
```

in the command prompt.

It is important to use single quotes to encapsulate the string. Escape characters such as \n can be used to insert non-printable characters to format the layout.

Variables can be inserted into the string, and they would be replaced by their respective values before being displayed. Place holder syntax for the variable depends on the data type.

Data type	Place holder character
Integer	%i
Double	%d
Float	%f
String	%s

Refer to the appendix for a more complete list. You can mix different variable types in the same string. A value for each place holder is stated after the string.

Example 1

```
    fprintf ('maximum height reached is %d
meters' , x);
```

%d would be replaced by the value in x variable before printing. If x is 23.91, the following would be printed

```
    maximum height reached is 23.91 meters
```

Example 2

```
    fprintf ('Voltage is %d voltd and Current
is %i Amperes' , x , y);
```

Note that %i is used as the second place holder. Therefore, the variable y must be of the integer type.

You may use extra parameters to format the string, such as changing the number of decimal places displayed.

Conditional Branching

So far, all the statements in the program have been executed in order. But sometimes it is necessary to execute a statement only under certain conditions. Such syntax is known as conditional executions. Most common syntax is called `if` condition. `if else` syntax allows selection between two sets of statements. Therefore, such syntax is called conditional branching. Another possible branching syntax is the `switch` syntax.

IF syntax

In programming terminology, we can use `if` condition to achieve conditional execution. Common syntax would be

```
If condition
        Statements to be executed, if the
condition is true
    end
```

Example

Think of a program that calculates the absolute value of a number. If the number is negative, we multiply it by -1.

Let x be the variable representing the number. The condition here is to check if the number is less than zero (x < 0). If the condition is true, we would do something, In this case multiply by minus one(x = x*-1).

Final syntax would be

```
if x < 0
    x = x*-1;
end
```

Let's modify the program so a person can enter a number through the keyboard.

```
x = input('please enter a number \n');

if x < 0
    x = x*-1;
end

fprintf ('absolute value is %d \n',x);
```

Exercise

1) Write a program to check if the number entered by the user is greater than 100. If so, display a warning.

2) Write a program to display a warning, if the value of x is negative.

Relational operators

Following is a set of relational operators, which can be used to test conditions

Operator	Example	Description
<	A < B	Is A less than B
>	A > B	Is A greater than B
<=	A <= B	Is A less than or equal to B

>=	A >= B	Is A greater than or equal to B
==	A == B	Is A equal to B
~=	A ~= B	Is A not equal to B

> **Important**
>
> *The operators <, >, <=, and >= use only the real part of their operands for the comparison. However, == and ~= use both real and imaginary parts.*

IF ELSE syntax

Another common scenario would be when we want to choose between two options, depending on the condition. This can be done by using two `if` conditions. However, a better alternative would be `if else` syntax.

```
if condition
      statements to be executed when
condition is true
    else
      statements to be executed when
condition is false
    end
```

Example

Let's write a program to determine if a student has passed or failed depending on the marks he obtained. Let the cutoff mark be 50. Then the program may look like

```
marks = input('Please enter the marks \n');
if marks >= 50
    fprintf('Pass \n')
else
```

```
        fprintf('fail \n')
    end
```

First statement prompts user for marks. The number entered would be assigned to a variable called marks.

Then the condition (`marks > 50`) is checked.

If the condition is true, i.e. marks is equal or greater than 50, the first set of statements is executed `fprintf('Pass \n')`. Statements under else condition are ignored.

If the condition is false, i.e. marks is less than 50, then only the statements under else condition is executed `fprintf('fail \n')`.

TIP

> Note that the comparator used in the above example is >= , which means greater than or equal to. If we only used >, a student getting marks of 50 would be considered failed.

Exercise

1) Write a MATLAB program to prompt the user for room temperature. If the value is less than 10, display "It is cold".

2) How do you modify the above program to print a second statement, "it is hot", if the temperature is above 35.

Logical operators

Logical operators can be used to concatenate multiple conditions together.

Syntax

```
(Condition 1) operator (Condition 2)
operator (Condition)
```

Syntax	Details	Example
&	And operator	A > 0 & B < 100
|	Or operator	A > 0 | B < 100

Example

A student is considered passed if he got more than 50 marks for the written paper and more than 75 marks for the practical assessment. Implement a program to calculate if a student has passed the exam.

There are two conditions to pass the exam. The first condition is about the written paper (written_marks > 50). The second condition is about the practical assessments (practical_marks > 75). Both of these conditions need to be satisfied to pass the exam. Therefore, they are concatenated using the "and" condition.

```
written_marks = input('Enter written exam
marks \n');
```

```
    practical_marks = input('Enter the
practical exam marks \n');

    if written_marks > 50 & practical_marks >
75
        fprintf('Passed \n');
    else
        fprintf('Failed \n');
    end
```

Example

A person is diagnosed with a particular disease if chemical A in his blood falls below 30 or chemical B rises above 50. Write a program for the above scenarios.

```
A = input('Chemical A \n');
B = input('Chemical B \n');

if A < 30 | B > 50
    fprintf('Sick \n');
else
    fprintf('Healthy \n');
end
```

It is possible to have more than one logical operator

Example

```
if (A < 30 & B > 50 ) | C < 30
    fprintf('Conditions are met \n');
else
    fprintf('Conditions are not met \n' );
end
```

We can make the grouping of the logical operator using parentheses.

Nested if

It is possible to include one if condition inside another if condition. This is called 'nesting'.

Example

In the following example, nested if conditions are used to check two conditions one after another.

```
if Attendance > 50
        if Marks > 75
      fprintf('Pass \n');
end
else
      fprintf('Failed \n');
end
```

Exercises

1) Rewrite the program of diagnosing a patient, which was provided in the previous example, using nested if,

Loop Structures

Sometimes it is required to repeat the same statement. Two common methods are `for` structure and `while` structure. Each repletion is called an iteration.

for structure is used when the number of repetitions is predetermined. while structure is used when the number of repetitions is unknown and is determined later by a condition.

For loop structure

Let us try to print "Hello world" a hundred times on the command line. Since the number of repetition is known, for structure is used

Syntax

```
for index = 1:number_of_repetitions
    repeating_statements
end
```

Example

```
for j = 1:100
    disp('Hello world') % we can also use
fprintf command
    end
```

The loop starts by setting j to 1. At the end of each iteration, j is incremented by one. Therefore, the variable j is called an incrementing variable. Before the start of each iteration, the incrementing variable is compared with the upper limit of iteration. If the incrementing variable is larger repetition is stopped. This is called the termination of the 'for loop'. In each iteration, it is possible to access the incrementing variable.

Example

```
for i = 1:5
```

```
        disp (i);
    end
```

Result

```
    1
    2
    3
    4
    5
```

It is possible to change the starting value, the ending value, or the size of increments.

Example

In the following, iteration would start from 5 and continue to 8

```
for i = 5:8
        disp (i);
    end
```

Result

```
    5
    6
    7
    8
```

Example

In the following, increment step size is increased to 2

```
for i = 1:2:10
    disp (i);
end
```

Example

In the following iteration, we start from 10 and decrement with 0.5 steps to 6.

```
for i = 10:-0.5:6
    disp (i);
end
```

Example

Print all the odd numbers from 1 to 100. Here we start from 1 and move up to 100. Since we want odd numbers, the step size is 2.

```
for i = 1:2:100
    disp (i);
end
```

One of the most useful functions of for loop is the access to matrix or array elements.

```
marks = [83,10,55,10,43];
for i = 1:2:10
    disp (i);
end
```

Let's make changes so the marks of the students are printed along with the pass status.

```matlab
marks = [83,10,55,10,43]; % List of marks
for i = 1:5
    current_mark= marks(i); % select a
value
    if current_mark > 50   % decide on a
message
        fprintf('student %i passed \n',i)
    else
        fprintf('student %i failed \n',i)
    end
end
```

Nested for loops

Like the nested if conditions, it is possible to nest loop structures.

Example

Following implementation, access each element in a 2D matrix.

```matlab
A = magic(10)
for i=1:10
    for j = 1:10
        A(i,j)
    end
end
```

While loops

A while loop continues repetition until a condition is false.

Syntax

```
While condition
repeating statements
end
```

Example

In the following code, we would start from 10 and continue to divide it by 2 until it is less than 0.1;

```
x = 10;
while x > 0.1
    x = x /2
end
```

Breaking from a loop

Sometimes it is required to break from a loop suddenly. Break is used for that purpose.

Example

Print the marks in the array. However, if any of the marks are negative, immediately exit from the loop.

```
Marks = [8, 3, 6, -8 , 10, 8];
for m = 1:5
    Marks(m)
    if  Marks(m) < 0
        break
    end
end
```

When the loop reaches the negative mark, break is triggered. The looping stops.

In case of a nested loop, it will only exit the loop that includes the break statement.

Skipping an iteration

Sometimes it is required to skip only a single iteration. When the keyword continue is encountered, the rest of the loop is omitted and the loop moves to next iteration.

```
Marks = [8, 3, 6, -8 , 10, 8];
for m = 1:5

    if  Marks(m) < 0
        continue
    end
      Marks(m)
end
```

When the loop reaches the negative mark, that iteration is skipped and moves to the next number.

MATLAB Functions

Introduction

By now, you should be familiar enough to program some of your own ideas in MATLAB. Perhaps you are already trying out some of your research or educational projects on it. But very soon you will notice a few things.

As the problems get more complex, the codes become more complex as well! They soon become so long and confusing that you will find it difficult to make out what each line is doing. If you dig up a code from your last week's work to make just one minor change, it may become a nightmare. You cannot make head or tails out of some of your own codes. (Comments and good variable names can help mitigate the problem, but not completely eliminate it). Sometimes you need to repeat the same task in multiple locations of the code and it's not only boring and time consuming, it is also confusing. Very soon, you start to wonder if there is a better way to do this. Fortunately, there is! It is called using functions.

Remember how you did your last big project? You first divided it into smaller manageable chunks and worked on each of these smaller problems. This is called divide and conquer, and it is the concept behind functions.

One of the main reasons for all your problems is a lack of hierarchical organization in the code. All the statements are written into the same big script file. To make life easier, we will break this large script into a set of smaller components. These smaller, self-contained components are called functions. Ideally a function should perform one and only one task.

It is like building a block diagram. At the higher levels you are only concerned about the overall design. You don't bother about small details. Once the task is broken into blocks, you can take one block at a time and focus on building it.

Think of the following hypothetical scenario. A company manufactures paper weights. They can be made from wood, glass, or ceramics. Their shape can be cylindrical, semi-hemispherical or cubical. The total cost is determined by the volume of material used, and the amount of surface area that needs to be polished. How do you write a program to calculate this?

Generic Function Syntax

```
function [output_ 1, output_ 2,...] =
function_name (input_ 1, input_ 2, input_ 3....)
```

> **Important**
>
> *Each function should be on its own script file. The name of the script file should be same as the function name. You need to assign your result to the output variables.*
> *Function names cannot have spaces or begin with a number. You should not use existing standard MATLAB function names as your function names.*
> *Your function script file and the main file should be in the same folder*

Data exchange with the function

As you may remember, scripts share the MATLAB workspace. They can access any variable in the workspace. They can also edit or create new variables on the MATLAB workspace. So you can create a variable x in one script and use it in another script. However, functions act differently.

Each function has its own enclosed unique workspace. If a variable x is created inside a function, it cannot be seen by other functions or scripts. This is similar to how a function cannot see any of the variables in the MATLAB workspace. The only way to exchange data with a function is by passing parameters through the header.

Any value you want to send into the function is called an input parameter and is inside the parentheses. Results coming from the function are called the output parameters and are inside the brackets. It is important to preserve the order of parameters as assigned.

Example 1

Create a function that takes radius as the input parameter and output area.

```
function [area] = calc_area(radius)
area = pi*radius^2;
```

Here, the input parameter is radius. We can write the code, as we already know the value of the radius. Because at the time of function call radius variable would be replaced by that value. After the calculation, the final answer is assigned to the output variable area.

Save the above code in a separate script file named calc_area.m

In your main file, you can call the above function as follows

```
clear
clc

calc_area(5)
```

Here, the calc area function is called with input parameter 5. Calculations inside the function are carried out by replacing the variable radius with the value 5.

The result is

```
ans =
    78.5398
```

We can reuse the function

```
area_small_circle = calc_area(2);
area_average_circle = calc_area(7);
area_large_circle =calc_area(12);
```

This would calculate the area of three separate circles and assign it to the given three variables.

Example 2

Create a function to calculate the volume of a cylinder. Radius and height of the cylinder is provided.

Here we have two input parameters radius and height.

```
function [volume] =
calc_volume(radius,height)
    volume = pi*radius^2*height;
```

The above function needs to be save in a file called `calc_volume.m`

It can be called using

```
calc_volume(3,5)
```

and the result is

```
ans   =
141.3717
```

Inside a function, you can have many complex statements. For example, look at the following function which calculates the factorial of a given number.

```
function [value] = calc_factorial(n)

if n == 0
    value = 1;
else
    k = 1;
    for i = 1:n
        k = k*i;
    end
    value = k;
end
```

Multiple outputs

Theoretically, you can have only a single output from a function. But this output can be of any type, including matrices. Therefore, it is possible to have multiple value outputs from a function.

Example

Let's create a function to calculate the volume and surface area of a cube.

```
function [properties] = cube_properties(h)
area = 6*h^2;
volume = h^3;
properties = [area , volume];
```

We can call the function as follows
```
Prop = cube_properties(3)
```

The result is

```
prop
=
    54      27
```

Recursion

Recession is a special way of defining a function. It may seem little confusing at first, however, in certain scenarios, recursion provides the most efficient solutions.

Recursion can be stated as defining a function using itself. In other words, inside the body of the function is a call to the function itself. The most important rule in recursive function is that it needs to terminate after a finite number of steps.

Example

The factorial of a number can be calculated using following formula

$$n! = 1 \times 2 \times 3 \, ... \, n$$

By above definition

$$5! = 1 \times 2 \times 3 \times 4 \times 5$$

It's possible to write

$$5! = (1 \times 2 \times 3 \times 4) \times 5 = 4! \times 5$$

In general

$$n! = (n-1)! \times n$$

The only exception is 0! = 1 which is a mathematical fact.

We can write the above as a function

```
function [result] = calc_factorial (n)
result = calc_factorial(n-1)*n;
```

During the function call, we pass a number for n (e.g. 5). Inside the function, n is replaced by this value. Part of the statement call to the function itself, `calc_factorial`, But now the value we pass is reduced by 1 (e.g. 4). Likewise, every time function is called, it is reduced by 1.

It is important to do a termination condition. In this case we can say 1! = 1. So we do not need to call the function again to calculate 1!.

Final function would be

```
function [result] = calc_factorial (n)

if n == 1
    result = 1;
```

```
else
    result = calc_factorial(n-1)*n;
end
```

Let us see what happens when we call

```
calc_factorial(4)
```

Since n is not 1, calc_factorial(3) is called.

Inside the calc_factorial(3), calc_factorial(2) is called. Inside calc_factorial(2), calc_factorial(1) is called. Now the n is 1. Therefore, the termination condition is satisfied. Instead of calling calc_factorial again, it passes result 1 to its caller. calc_factorial(2) receives the result and its result, 2, is sent back to its parent calc_factorial(3). Using the results from calc_factorial(2), factorial 3 is calculated and sent to its parent. Finally, calc_factorial(4) uses the answer from calc_factorial(3) to provide the final result.

This can be explained using a figure as follows

// Image explaining the factorial unraveling

1	recursiveFunction (0)				
2		recursiveFunction (0+1)			
3			recursiveFunction (1+1)		
4				recursiveFunction (2+1)	
5					recursiveFunction (3+1)
6					printf (4)
7				printf (3)	
8			printf (2)		
9		printf (1)			
10	printf (0)				

Chapter 5 :
Symbolic Mathematics

Sometimes it is necessary to work with generic equations that are based on symbols. For example, vertical displacement of a free-falling object is described using

$$s = ut + \frac{gt^2}{2}$$

If we want to find S and the values of all the other variables are known, it is easy to solve. But assume instead that we want a generic expression for its speed. Now, our result is another mathematical expression, not a number. To get this expression, we need to differentiate the above equation. For most computer languages, this is an impossible task. They are designed to calculate based on numbers. But not for MATLAB. MATLAB has the ability to evaluate mathematical symbols, which is quite useful. In this chapter we will learn how to use the symbolic toolbox.

Initializing Symbolic Variables

So far, we have seen that MATLAB automatically determines the type of the variable. But now, we explicitly want to say that the following is a symbolic variable and treat it as such

Syntax

```
syms   'list of symbolic variables'
```

The symbolic variable name must start with a letter and can only contain alphanumeric characters.

Example

syms x t y

The above command will create three symbolic variables named x , y and t. It is important not to use commas to separate variables. In the workspace, new variables will have a small cube as an icon. Their value would be the dimension followed by the postfix sym.

Adding assumptions

Sometimes these variables are accompanied by assumptions, such as x is a real number. It is possible to add these assumptions for the variables.

```
syms 'list of variables'   assumptions
```

Example

```
syms x y real
```

This would create two symbolic variables named x,y and assume they are real numbers.

Creating mathematical functions

If the expression of interest is lengthy or needs to be used multiple times, it is convenient to create a symbolic function

Example

create the following two functions

$$f(x) = x^2 + \sin(x)$$
$$h(x, y) = \sin(x)^2 + y^2$$

Syntax

```
syms x y
f(x) = x^2 + sin(x)
h(x,y) = sin(x)^2 + y^2
```

you can call a symbolic function by its name e.g.

```
>> h
h(x, y) =
cos(x)^2 + y^2
```

Evaluating a symbolic function

There are three levels of presentation for a mathematical formula:
Level 1:

This is the most abstract level with each variable represented by a symbol.

e.g. $f(x) = x^2 + \sin(x)$

Example

```
syms x
f(x) = x^2 + sin(x)
```

The symbolic toolbox is used most in this area. We shall learn more later in this chapter.

Level 2:
Numerical values of the parameters are known. Some of the terms may be evaluated to a number without the loss of accuracy. Other terms are kept as symbols, however.

E.g.
$$f(x) = x^2 + \sin(x)$$
$$f(3)$$

Example

```
syms x;
f(x) = x^2 + sin(x);
f(3)
```

The result is

```
>> Sin(3) + 9
```

It is clear that x^2 can be evaluated to 9 without loss of accuracy. But evaluating sin(3) may result in loss of accuracy. Therefore, that term is kept as a symbol.
Following is a more interesting example

$$f(x) = 2x + \sqrt{x}$$

Code

```
syms x;
f(x) = 2*x + sqrt(x);
```

substituting x = 4 we get

```
>> f(4)
>> 10
```

However, if we set x = 2 we get

```
>>f(2)
>> 2^(1/2) + 4
```

This is because $\sqrt{2}$ is irrational and cannot be accurately represented by a finite number of digits.

Level 3:

This is the level where we want to force a number as the result. For example, we are designing an antenna and its length is calculated using a complex formula. But when all is said and done, you want a number which can be measured using a meter ruler.

Syntax

```
eval (expression)
```

Example

$$f(x) = x^2 + \sin(x)$$
$$f(3) = ?$$

Code

```
syms x;
f(x) = x^2 + sin(x);
eval(f(3))
```

the result would be

```
ans =
     9.1411
```

Expanding an Expression

If we want to expand a formula, we can use the following syntax

Syntax

```
expand('expression')
```

Example 1

expand the following expression
$$f(x) = (x + 3)^3$$

Code

```
syms x;
f(x) = (x+3)^3;
expand(f)
```

Result

```
ans(x) =
x^3 + 9*x^2 + 27*x + 27
```

Example 2

In the following example, we are using three variables.

Expand
$$(x + 1)(y + z)$$

Code

Instead of defining a function in a separate statement, it is defined inside the expand function itself. Note that no single quotes are used inside the expand function.

```
syms x y z
expand((x + 1)*(y + z))
```

Result

```
ans =
y + z + x*y + x*z
```

Further reading

- A second parameter can be passed to expand the command to limit the depth of expansion.

Simplify an Expression

An expression can be simplified using the following command

Syntax

```
simplify('expression')
```

Example

Simplify
$$\sin{(x)}^2 + \cos{(x)}^2$$

Code

```
syms x;
simplify(sin(x)^2 + cos(x)^2)
```

Result

```
      ans
  = 1
```

Exercise

Simplify the following expressions

1. $x^2 + y^2 + 2xy$
2. $x^2 + y^2 - 2xy$
3.

Further reading

- What are the extra parameters that can be passed to simplify the command

Solving Equations

Equations are found in many mathematical models. By using the solve command, they can be solved easily.

Solving single variable equations

Syntax

solve(equation)

Example

We want to find the solution for $x^2 + 2x = 15$

Code

```
syms x
solve(x^2 + 2*x == 15)
```

Note that to represent the equal sign in the mathematical equation, two assignation marks (==) are used in the code.

result

```
ans =
   3
  -5
```

Example 2

We want to find the solution for $\sin(x) = \cos(x)$ for the first quadrant.

Code

```
syms x
solve(cos(x) == sin(x) )
```

The result

```
ans =
pi/4
```

Solving multiple variable equations

If the equation has more than one variable, the result may include them in the answer. You can specify which variable you want to solve by the second argument.

Syntax

solve(equation, variable to solve)

Example1

We want to find the value of x in the *expression* $x^2 + 2x = y + 1$

Code

```
syms x y
solve(x^2 + 2*x == y + 1 ,x )
```

Result

```
ans =
   (y + 2)^(1/2) - 1
 - (y + 2)^(1/2) - 1
```

There are two possible values for x. both of them contain the variable y.

Example 2

We want to find the value of y in the expression $x^2 + 2x = y + 1$

```
syms x y
```

```
solve(x^2 + 2*x == y + 1 ,y )
```

result

```
ans =
x^2 + 2*x - 1
```

There is only one possible solution for y.

Solving simultaneous equations

If there is a set of equations that describes the same set of variables, it is called a set of simultaneous equations.
E.g.

$$2x - y = 1$$
$$x - 3y = -8$$

Syntax

solve(equation 1, equation 2,… equation n)

However, the result of the above command is given as a structure. To find the value of a given variable, we need to drill into the structure using '.' command.

Syntax

```
sol = solve(equation 1, equation 2,…
equation n);
sol.varaible_name
```

Example1

We want to find the value of x and y in the following simultaneous equations

$$2x - y = 1$$
$$x - 3y = -8$$

Code

```
syms x y;
sol = solve(2*x - y == 1, x - 3*y == 8);
x_value = sol.x
y_value = sol.y
```

We have assigned the value of x and y to two other variables named x_value and y_value.

Result

```
x_value =
-1

y_value =
-3
```

Example 2

We want to find the value of x and y in the following simultaneous equations

$$2x - y + z = 1$$
$$x - 3y - z = -8$$
$$y + z = 0$$

Code

```
syms x y z;
sol = solve(2*x - y + z== 1, x - 3*y -z==
8, y+z == 0);
    x_value = sol.x
    y_value = sol.y
    z_value = sol.z
```

Result

```
x_value =
-7

y_value =
 -15/2

z_value =
 15/2
```

Example 3

We want to find the values of x and y in the following simultaneous equations. Note that the equations are under constraint and that the first equation is a polynomial.

$$x^2 = y$$
$$y + z = 9$$

Code

```
syms x y z;
sol = solve(x^2 == y, y + z == 9 );
x_value = sol.x
y_value = sol.y
```

Result

```
x_value =
   (9 - z)^(1/2)
  -(9 - z)^(1/2)


y_value =
   9 - z
   9 - z
```

Differentiation

Differentiation is a very important tool. MATLAB provides analytical and numerical differentiation tools.

Differentiation with single variable

By default, MATLAB differentiates a function with respect to x.

Syntax

diff('function')

Example 1

Let $f(x) = x^2 + \sin(x)$ Find $\frac{d(f(x))}{dx}$

Code

```
syms x
f(x) = x^2 + sin(x);
diff(f)
```

Result

```
ans(x) =
2*x + cos(x)
```

Example 2

It is possible to directly type the function into the diff command.

```
syms x
diff(x^2 + sin(x))
```

Partial Derivatives.

When we have more than one symbolic variable in the expression, we can pass a second parameter. Expression would be differentiated with respect to the variable in this second parameter.

Syntax

diff('function', diff with respect to this variable)

Example 1

Let $f(x, y, z) = x^2y + \sin(z) + \dfrac{y}{2z}$ Find $\dfrac{d(f)}{dx}$

Code

```
syms x y z;
f(x,y,z) = x^2*y + sin(z) + y/(2*z);
diff(f,x)
```

Result

ans(x, y, z) =

2*x*y

Example 2

Let's differentiate the same example with respect to z

$$f(x,y,z) = x^2 y + \sin(z) + \frac{y}{2z} \quad \text{Find} \quad \frac{d(f)}{dz}$$

Code

```
syms x y z;
f(x,y,z) = x^2*y + sin(z) + y/(2*z);
diff(f,z)
```

Result

```
ans(x, y, z) =
```

cos(z) - y/(2*z^2)

Higher order derivatives

We can obtain higher order derivatives by repeating the diff command multiple times. However, a much easier approach is to pass order as a parameter.

Syntax

diff('function', order)

Example 1

Let $f(x,y,z) = x^2 y + \sin(z)$ Find $\dfrac{d(f)^2}{dx^2}$

Code

```
syms x y z;
f(x,y,z) = x^2*y + sin(z);
diff(f,x,2)
```

Result

```
ans(x, y, z) =
2*y
```

Further readings

Learn how to use gradient, curl and divergence functions.

Integration

Since we have learned the basics of using MATLAB for differentiation, let's learn how to integrate.

Indefinite integration

By default, MATLAB integrates a function with respect to x.

Syntax

int('function')

Example 1

Let $f(x) = x^2y + \sin(x)$ Find $\int f(x).dx$

Code

```
syms x
f(x)  =   x^2 + sin(x);
int(f)
```

Result

```
     ans(x)  =
y*(sin(x)  + x^2)
```

Example 2

Let $f(x) = log_e(x) + \frac{1}{x}$ Find $\int f(x).dx$

In MATLAB, a natural logarithm is represented by log()

Code

```
syms x
f(x)  =   log(x) + 1/x;
int(f)
```

Result

```
ans(x)  =
log(x)  - x + x*log(x)
```

Selecting integrating variable

When multiple symbolic variables are present, we may wish to change the integrating variable. This can be done by passing it as the second parameter

Syntax

int('function',integrating variable)

Example 1

Let $f(x) = x + sin(xy) + y$ Find $\int f(x,y).dx$

Code

```
syms x y
f(x) =  x + sin(x*y)+ y;
int(f,x)
```

Result

```
    ans(x) =
x*y + x^2/2 - cos(x*y)/y
```

Example 2

Let's try to integrate the same function, but with respect to y.

Let $f(x) = x + \sin(xy) + y$ Find $\int f(x,y).dy$

Code

```
syms x y
f(x) =  x + sin(x*y)+ y;
int(f,y)
```

Result

```
    ans(x) =
x*y + y^2/2 - cos(x*y)/x
```

Definite integration

The interval of the integration can be passed into the int command, making it compute the definite integral.

Syntax

int('function', lower boundary, upper boundary)

Example 1

Let's try to integrate the following.
Let $f(x) = 2x$ Find $\int_2^5 f.dx$

Code

```
syms x
f(x)  =   2*x;
int(f,2,5)
```

Result

```
ans(x)  =
```
21

Example 1

Here, the upper boundary of the integration is a variable itself. But the syntax remains the same
Let $f(x) = 2x$ Find $\int_2^{5(z+1)} f.dx$

Code

```
syms x z
f(x)  =   2*x;
int(f,2,5*(z+1))
```

Result

```
ans(x)  =
(5*z + 5)^2 - 4
```

Chapter 6 : MATLAB plots

Plots are useful to represent complex data in a user-friendly manner. For example, it is easier to see something in a line graph than going through it in a table. MATLAB supports a wide array of graphs. These include, but are not limited to

- 2D and 3D line plots
- Pie charts
- Histograms
- Bar charts
- Scatter plots
- Surface and mesh plots

GUI for Plotting a Variable

If you just want a quick peek on to how a variable behaves, the easiest method would be to use the plot icons. But the skill of generating a plot using commands will pay off handsomely in the long run and developing it is highly recommended.

To plot a graph using GUI

1. Select the variable(s) you wish to plot from the work space. (Use shift key to select multiple variables)
2. Use PLOT tab to see the possible plotting options for selected variables
3. Click on the plot type.
4. The plot would appear in a new figure window.

5. To edit properties, such as axis names, use the edit menu in the figure window

Scripts on Plotting Graphs

There are two types of graphs.
- Analytical graphs
- Numerical graphs

Analytical graphs are based on functions. Functions are defined as relationships between two or more variables. An example is y = sin(x). Numerical graphs represent the discrete data points. For example, think of an experiment where you measure the temperature of water minute by minute as it is heated. If you measure it for 15 minutes, there will be 15 data points. These points can be marked and may be connected using a line.

Analytical Graphs

The easiest method to plot a function is to use the 'ezplot' command.

Syntax
```
ezplot ( 'function you need to plot' )
```

Example

Let's try to plot sin(2x)

```
ezplot ( 'sin(2*x)' )
```

Note the single double quotes surrounding the function. In other words, the function needs to be provided as a string. Another common mistake is to type sin(2x) instead of sin(2*x). If you need to multiply two terms, you need to put a multiplication sign in the middle.

The final result would be similar to the following figure:

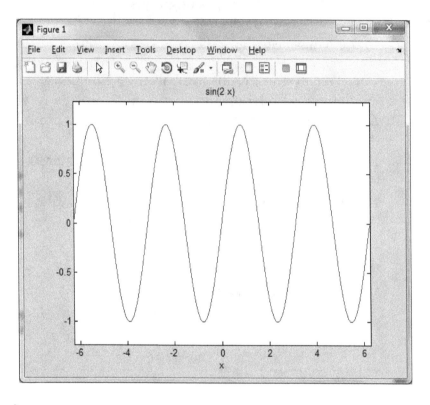

Exercise

Try plotting the following graphs
- $\cos(5x)$
- $\sin(2x) + x^2$
- $\text{Log}(x)$

Changing title and axis names

Let's start by changing the default title and the names of the x and y axes.

Syntax

ezplot ('function you need to plot'), title 'your title, xlabel 'name x axis', y label 'name y axis'.

Let's change the title, x axis name and y axis name to my signal, time and voltage respectively

```
ezplot('sin(2*x)'), title 'my signal' ,
xlabel 'time' , ylabel 'voltage'
```

All the graph attributes, such as title, are set after closing the parenthesis of the ezplot command.

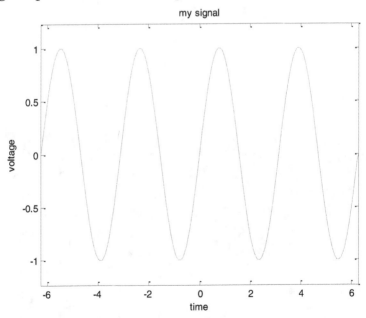

Changing axis scale

Default range for x is -2π to 2π. This can be changed using following command

```
ezplot('function',[x_min, x_max])
```

Example

```
ezplot('x^3' , [ -2 , 2])
```

If scaling of the y axis is also required, we need to add two extra parameters

```
Syntax
ezplot('function',[x_min, x_max, y_min , y_max])
```

```
Example
```

```
ezplot('x^3' , [ -2 , 2 , -10 10])
```

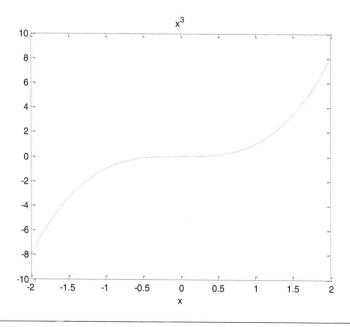

Plotting multiple variables

The ezplot command also supports multiple variables. For example, you can plot

```
ezplot('x^2 + y^2 = 9')
```

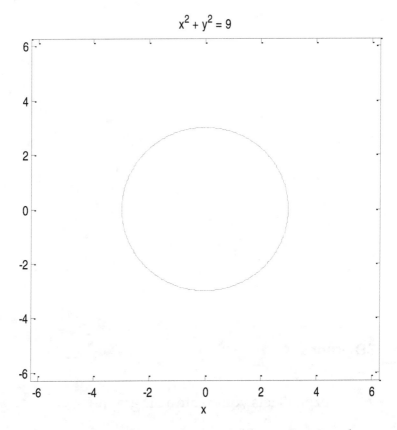

$$x^2 + y^2 = 9$$

It also supports plotting one variable against another

Syntax

```
ezplot('x function' , y function)
```

Example

x = sin(t)
y = cos(2t)

```
ezplot('sin(t)','cos(2*t)')
```

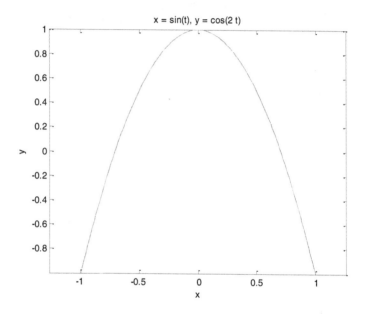

3D graphs

ezplot3 lets you create a 3D graph

Syntax

```
ezplot3('x function', 'y function', 'z
function')
```

Example

```
ezplot3('sin(2*t)', 'cos(2*t)', 't')
```

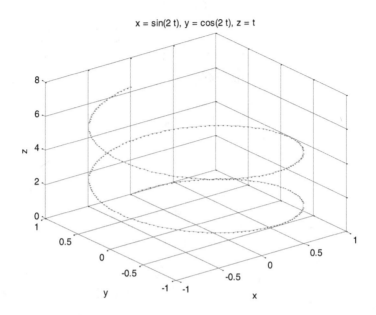

Rotating the graph

Click on the *rotate 3D* icon on the figure menu bar, At this point, the mouse pointer will change to a hand icon. Click and drag to rotate the graph in 3D.

Numerical Graphs

Numerical graphs are based on numbers or data points. For example, the following is a set of data for 12 consecutive points. Let's plot a line graph for it.

Start by creating a matrix for data

```
temperature = [27.1, 27.1, 27.3 ,27.5,
28.6, 29.2, 28.1, 28.6, 28.7,28.4, 27.0, 26.4]
```

Now, plot the data

Syntax

```
Plot(names of the variable)
```

Example

```
plot(temperature)
```

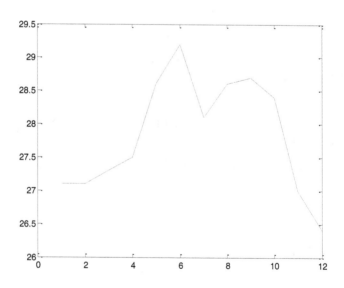

Plotting Y vs. X

```
Plot(names of the variable)
```

The command assumes that x values start from 1 and use increments of 1 for each pair. But this may not always be the case
- x may not always start form 1
- The difference between two consecutive points may not be 1
- Distance between data points may not be even

In this case, we can pass a second variable that contains the x axis values

Syntax

```
Plot(x variable name , y variable name)
```

Example

```
year = [1999 ,2000 ,2003, 2004 ,2008];
population = [1.23, 1.25, 1.5, 1.6, 1.62];
plot(year,population)
```

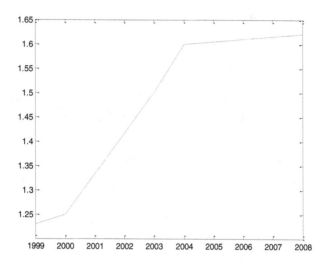

Axis labels and titles can be set using title, xlabel, ylabel commands.

```
plot(year,population),
title 'population growth in country x',
xlabel 'year' , ylabel 'population in
millions'
```

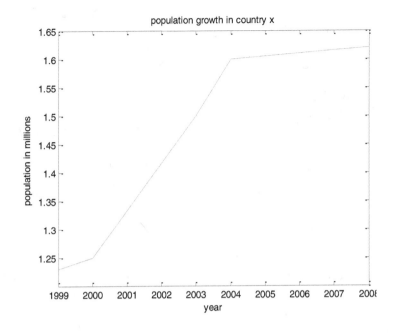

Graphing options

It is possible to change the color, marker, line width and many other attributes of the graph. (Refer to appendix for a more complete list)

Line color syntax

```
plot(variables, 'color code letter')
```

Color code letter	Color
g	green
r	red
c	cyan
m	magenta
y	yellow
k	black

w	white
b	blue

Example

The following would change the line color to red

```
plot(year,population,'r')
```

Data point style

Sometimes we need to show where data points were taken instead of the lines. For this use the following syntax
Syntax
```
plot(variables, 'data point style letter')
```

Data point style letter	Data point symbol
.	Point
O	Circle
x	x-mark
+	Plus
*	Star
(None)	No data points shown

(Refer to appendix for a more complete list)
The following example would mark data points using stars

```
plot(year,population,'*')
```

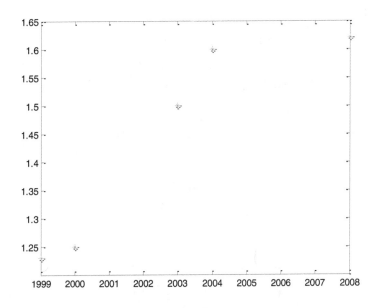

Line styles

You can change the style of the line. This is really useful if you have multiple trends plotted on the same graph. Syntax is as follows

```
plot(variables, 'line style letter')
```

Line style letter	Line style
-	Solid
:	Dotted
-.	Dash and dot
--	Dashed
(none)	No line

Example

```
plot(year,population,'--')
```

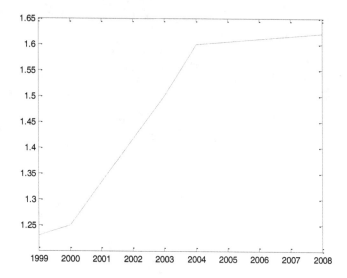

You can combine all the above attributes. For example, the following would plot the line in blue dash line and the data points would be shown as circles.

Example

```
plot(year,population,'b-o')
```

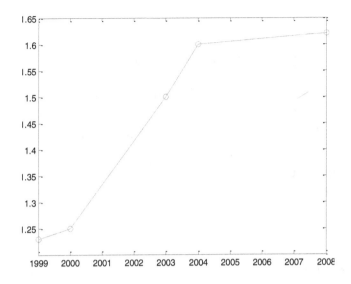

Multiple graphs

Now you know different methods for plotting graphs. However, you may notice that at any given time, there is only one graph is showing. Every time a new plot command is issued, new graphs are plotted on top of the old graph.

What if we want to look at multiple graphs at the same time?

There are three possible solutions

1. Show each graph in its own 'window'. (Technically this window is known as a figure window. It is the 'canvas' on which MATLAB draws images.)
2. Overlap graphs
3. Partition the same window and show a different graph in each section

Creating a new figure window

Graphical outputs, such as plots and images, are drawn in a special window called a figure window. By default, MATLAB draws all such drawings to the same default graph. Therefore, a new plot would overwrite the older plot. To create a new figure window, issue the 'figure' command. The next plot will be dawn in this new figure window

Example 1

```
x_1 = [120:-1:100];
y_1 =  sin(x_1);

x_2 = [-1 3 5 9 14];
y_2 =  [ 47 6 8 9 10];

plot(x_1,y_1);
figure;
plot(x_2,y_2);
```

Each time a figure command is issued, a new figure window is created. Since these are independent windows, they have their own menus and can be manipulated separately.

Example 2

```
dataset_1 = rand(1,10);
```

```
dataset_2 = rand(1,10);
dataset_3 = rand(1,10);

plot(dataset_1)
figure
plot(dataset_2)
figure
plot(dataset_3)
```

Overlap graphs

Sometimes graphs have a common variable and data need to be overlapped. This can be achieved by using the `hold` command. When hold is on, subsequent plotting commands add to the existing graph

Syntax

```
hold on
% over lapping figure elements
hold off
```

Example

```
x = [-5:0.1:5];
sine_curve = sin(x);
cos_curve = cos(x);
log_curve = log(x);

plot(x,sine_curve)
hold on
plot(x,cos_curve,'r--')
plot(x,log_curve,'m-.')
hold off
```

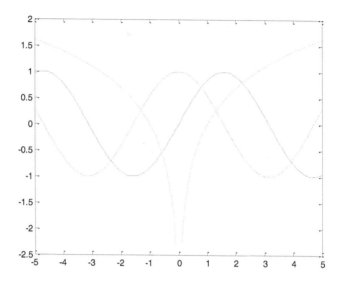

In the syntax lines have different styles. So they can be identified easier. However, adding a legend can help the user label each curve. To add a legend, use the following command after the last plotting command. The strings would be the label for each graph and they should be in the order of plotting.

Syntax

```
legend('string1','string2','string3', ...)
```

Example

```
plot(x,sine_curve)
hold on
plot(x,cos_curve, 'r--')
plot(x,log_curve, 'm-.')
```

```
    legend('sine function', 'cos function',
'log function')
    hold off
```

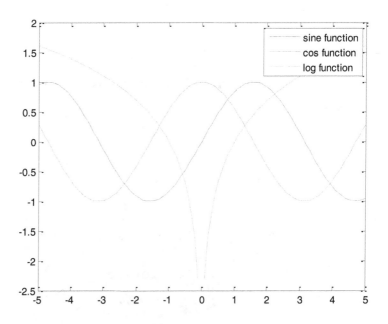

Sub Plots

When the parameters in the graphs are not identical, but are strongly correlated, we may wish to draw them side by side. This way, each graph would be independent enough to use its own scaling and plot type but close enough so users can compare them easily. The sub plot command allows multiple plots to be arranged inside a figure window in a tabular manner.

Syntax
subplot('total_rows', 'total columns' , 'location for current plot') ,
plot

Example

Let's plot sine curve and cosine curve in the same figure

```
x = [-5:0.1:5];
sine_curve = sin(x);
cos_curve = cos(x);

subplot(2,1,1), plot(sine_curve), title 'sine function'
subplot(2,1,2), plot(cos_curve), title 'cosine function'
```

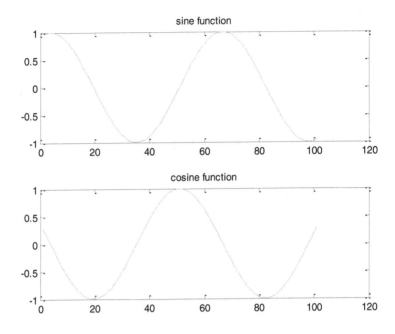

Example 2

In this example, charts are arranged in 2 by 2 manner defined by first two parameters in the subplot command) and there are four charts. 3rd parameter identify the location for each of them.

Example

```
subplot(2,2,1), ezplot('sin(x)')
subplot(2,2,2), hist(rand(10))
subplot(2,2,3), plot(rand(3,10))
subplot(2,2,4), ezplot('tan(x)')
```

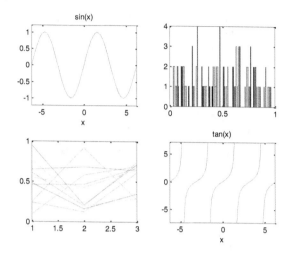

Exercise

So far, we have only considered line charts. There are many other chart types available in MATLAB. Here, we would learn some of the other commonly used chart types.

Bar graphs

Bar graphs is one of the most widely used plot types.

By default, each element in the array would be described using a single bar

Syntax

bar(data)

Example

```
data = [120 133 115 128 164 174]
bar(data)
```

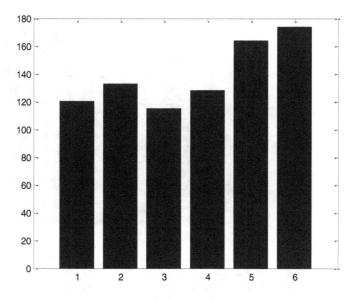

We can change the values in the x axis by using a second parameter

Syntax

```
bar(x_values, y_values)
```

Example

```
data = [120 133 115 128 164 174]
labels  = [110 120 130 140 150 160]
bar(labels,data)
```

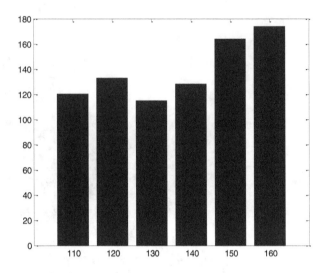

When the data is a 2D matrix, each row is considered to be a separate category

Histograms

Histograms are pictorial descriptions of how values are distributed. For example, think of marks obtained by the students in an exam. Let's categorize them into four groups, 0-25, 26-50, 51-75 and 76-100. Each of these group is called a *bin*. The number of students in each of these categories can be represented using a bar graph. Such a graph is known as a histogram.

It is possible to sort the data into bins manually or to use a MATLAB script and then use the bar chart to produce the histogram. However, MATLAB provides a single command that does all of that for you.

Syntax

```
hist(data)
```

Note: From the 2014b version, usage of `hist` syntax is discouraged and using the `histogram` command is recommended. Usage of the new command is similar in syntax

Example

```
data = rand(1,100);
hist(data)
```

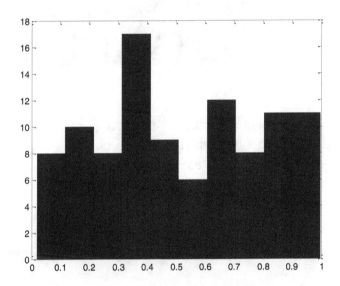

BY default, 10 bins are used. If a different number of bins is required, it can be passed as the second parameter.

Syntax

```
hist(data,number of bins)
```

Example

```
data = rand(1,100);
hist(data,4)
```

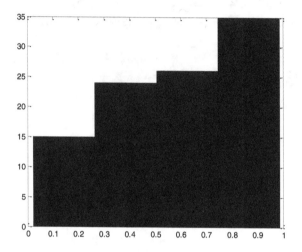

Another possible variation is when you wish to determine the boundaries of the classes. This is especially useful when bins have unequal value ranges.

Chapter 7 Moving Ahead

So far we have learned the basics of MATLAB. This should provide you with enough knowledge to continue.

Remember, practice makes perfect. The best way to learn MATLAB is by continuously practicing it and using it whenever possible.

We have only scratched the surface of this fascinating software. Here are some resources for you to learn more:

- MATLAB help file. This contains many examples and detailed descriptions.
- MATLAB forum. Use this online forum to get help from others. MATLAB has a very active and thriving community.
- MATLAB example videos

Appendix

Arithmetic Operators

Operator	Description
+	Addition
-	Subtraction
.*	Multiplication
./	Right division
.\	Left division
+	Unary plus
-	Unary minus
:	Colon operator
.^	Power
.'	Transpose
'	Complex conjugate transpose
*	Matrix multiplication
/	Matrix right division
\	Matrix left division
^	Matrix power

MATLAB data types

Data type	Details
double	double precision
single	single precision
int8	8-bit signed integer
int16	16-bit signed integer
int32	32-bit signed integer

int64	64-bit signed integer
uint8	8-bit unsigned integer
uint16	16-bit unsigned integer
uint32	32-bit unsigned integer
uint64	64-bit unsigned integer
char	Characters

Operator Precedence

1. Parentheses ()

2. Transpose (.'), power (.^), complex conjugate transpose ('), matrix power (^)

3. Unary plus (+), unary minus (-), logical negation (~)

4. Multiplication (.*), right division (./), left division (.\), matrix multiplication (*), matrix right division (/), matrix left division (\)

5. Addition (+), subtraction (-)

6. Colon operator (:)

7. Less than (<), less than or equal to (<=), greater than (>), greater than or equal to (>=), equal to (==), not equal to (~=)

8. Element-wise AND (&)

9. Element-wise OR (|)

10. Short-circuit AND (&&)

11. Short-circuit OR (||)

Escape characters

Function	Characters to type
Single quotation mark	''
Percent character	% %
Backslash	\\
Alarm	\a
Backspace	\b
Form feed	\f
New line	\n
Carriage return	\r
Horizontal tab	\t
Vertical tab	\v
Hexadecimal number, N	\xN
Octal number, N	\N

Statements

Most of the time in MATLAB, each statement is written on a separate line. This provides clarity and readability. But an advanced user may wish to change this behavior.

If a statement is too long you can continue it to the next line by using three dots at the end of first line.

If you wish to put several statements onto the same line, use semicolon as a termination symbol.

Example

```
A = [ 1 2 3 ...    % Statement continues to
next line
        4 5 6]
```

```
B = 4; D = 6    % Multiple statements on the same
line
```

About the Author

Gayan Illeperuma obtained his first degree in computational physics at the university of Colombo, followed by the Bachelor of Information Technology degree offered by the School of Computing at the University of Colombo. For his Ph.D. he studied on robot navigation have given him a strong background in artificial intelligence, computer vision, and robotics.

He formerly worked as a research scientist at Industrial Technology Institute of Sri Lanka. Later, he joined the University of Colombo as an academic and has conducted many courses and practical classes in MATLAB, Simulink, Programming, and Informatics. Many of the undergraduate and postgraduate research projects under his supervision have a strong MATLAB component. He is currently working as a Senior lecturer in the Open University of Sri Lanka, where he is researching open and long-distance learning methods for teaching student programming.

Discover MATLAB in 4 hours...

There are times when you want to get data analyzed quickly or to create a small program to get something done, but you do not have enough time to learn everything from the bottom up. If this is the case for you, you have found the best book for this purpose.

This book is designed to teach you the most important and most frequently used techniques of MATLAB in a very short period of time.

It will teach you how to
- Get start with MATLAB GUI
- Write MATLAB programs
- Use symbolic mathematics
- Plot figures and graphs

Each chapter of the book starts with simple examples and gradually increase in complexity. Each section is accompanied by important theories, background information, and exercises. Sections also include further references and exceptions for further explorations.

www.ingramcontent.com/pod-product-compliance
Lightning Source LLC
LaVergne TN
LVHW051700050326
832903LV00032B/3929